...IF YOU LIVED AT THE TIME OF
Martin Luther King

by Ellen Levine
illustrated by Anna Rich

SCHOLASTIC INC.
New York   Toronto   London   Auckland   Sydney

In memory of Fannie Lou Hamer.
And for Gloria Mims, from whom
I first learned about Mississippi.

With grateful thanks to Dean Haywood Burns, City University of New York Law School;
Professor Alan Gartner, Sponsored Research and Project Planning, City University of New York
Graduate Center; and Aviva Futorian, Esq., Director, Women's Law Project, Chicago, Illinois.
Thanks also to Sara Bullard, Research Director, Southern Poverty Law Center, Montgomery,
Alabama, for the Center's material about the Civil Rights Memorial Project.

ISBN 0-590-42582-X

12 11 10 9 8 7 6 5 4 3 2   4 5 6 7 8 9/9

Printed in the U.S.A.   08

First Scholastic printing, January 1994

Book design by Laurie McBarnette

CONTENTS

Introduction

Black people were brought to America from Africa as slaves. By the 1800s there were about four million slaves who lived and worked in the South. At the end of the Civil War in 1865, the slaves were freed. Many people thought that black Americans would then be treated equally and fairly.

But that didn't happen. Many whites all over the country continued to discriminate against black people. Southern states passed laws that kept most blacks poor and separated from whites. Sometimes people were put in jail or even killed if they broke these laws.

In the 1950s and 1960s, black people throughout the South began to get together to fight for their rights as free people. Martin Luther King, Jr., was one of the most famous leaders of this movement for change, known as the civil rights movement.

This book tells what it was like during those years of change in the South from 1955 until 1968, when Martin Luther King died. It is the story of blacks and their white supporters working together to make a better world for themselves and their children.

What was segregation?

Segregation was a whole way of life that white people set up to keep blacks and whites separated from each other. There were segregation laws and customs that kept the races apart. When Martin Luther King, Jr., was born in 1929, he was born into a segregated world.

Like most blacks, Martin Luther King lived in the South. He grew up in the city of Atlanta, Georgia. But it didn't matter whether you lived in the city or country, or how much money your family had. Southern laws said that blacks were to be segregated from whites.

Segregation laws were meant to make black people feel inferior to, or not as good as, whites. But white people didn't only use laws to make black people feel inferior. They often treated blacks in a rude way. For example, no matter how old a black man was, many whites would call him "boy." Black women as well as men were frequently called by their first names only. This was a way for whites not to show respect for blacks.

Martin Luther King, Jr., always remembered the day he first heard his father called "boy." Martin was a child. He was in a car with his father. A police officer stopped the car and said to Martin's father, "Show me your license, boy." The elder King looked at the officer and pointed to young Martin. "The child is a *boy*. I am a *man*."

Did black and white children go to different schools?

Yes. Throughout the South, schools were segregated. More money was spent for white schools. And so school segregation meant that black schools weren't as good as those for whites.

School conditions were even worse outside the cities. In many rural areas, children had to walk miles on dirt roads to get to school. Their schools were usually one-room buildings that were run-down. They were freezing in winter, hot in summer. Few of them had running water. Most had no electricity. The bathrooms were outdoors in little huts called out-houses.

It was hard for black children in the country to get a good education when there were few books, few teachers, few supplies, and such run-down buildings.

Did black and white children play together?

Sometimes, when they were very little. But as they grew up, their worlds became more and more segregated. By age six or seven, they were no longer allowed to be friends.

In one city there was even a law that blacks and whites could not play checkers or dominoes together.

Martin Luther King, Jr., had just started elementary school when he had to stop playing with his white friends. He and his friends went to different schools. One day when he went to his friends' house, their parents sent him away and told him not to come back. When he grew up he remembered that moment very clearly. He said that was when he first learned that some white people didn't think black people were as good as they were.

What else was segregated?

When Martin Luther King was growing up in the 1930s and 1940s, and into the 1950s, almost all public places in the South were segregated by law. If you walked out of your house or apartment, any place you could think of was probably segregated.

Everywhere you would see signs: WHITES ONLY, or COLORED ONLY, or NO NEGROES.

At the movies, black people had to sit in the back and usually upstairs. Sometimes they had to go to separate black theaters.

White people could get on a bus, put their money in the box, and take a seat. Blacks in many cities climbed aboard buses and put their money in. Then they had to leave the bus and get on again through the back door.

When you went to the doctor or dentist, whites waited in one room; blacks had to wait in a separate, smaller room. Blacks and whites sat at separate lunch counters and went to separate restrooms. They even had to drink at separate water fountains.

There were white restaurants and black restaurants, white hotels and black hotels, white elevators and black elevators, and separate public beaches.

If you were black and you were sick, you went to a black hospital. And when you died, you were buried in a black cemetery.

If your parents were soldiers in World War II in the 1940s, they fought against one enemy. But black soldiers and white soldiers slept in separate places and ate at different tables.

In Oklahoma there were segregated telephone booths. In South Carolina, black and white cotton mill workers were forbidden to look out the same window. And in Birmingham, Alabama, the public library wouldn't let anyone read a children's book showing black and white rabbits playing together.

What did the government say about segregation?

For many years, city and state governments and even the United States government said that nothing was wrong with segregation. There were segregation laws in states throughout the South.

In Louisiana in the 1890s, a law said that trains had to have separate cars for blacks and whites. One day a black man named Homer Plessy bought a train ticket in that state. He refused to sit in the "colored" car. Lawyers argued the case before the Supreme Court, the highest court in the United States. There are nine Justices on the Court. Eight said that there *could* be separate train cars for blacks and whites, as long as the cars were equal.

This became the law for the whole United States — and the law was that *everything*, not just train cars, could be separate, as long as it was equal. One Supreme Court Justice, John Marshall Harlan, disagreed. He said, "Our Constitution is color-blind."

Twelve years later, the National Association for the Advancement of Colored People, known by its initials, NAACP, was formed. The group believed that Justice Harlan was right. NAACP lawyers brought court cases to challenge segregation. Finally in 1954, fifty-eight years after the Plessy case, the Supreme Court changed its mind.

What happened in 1954?

In that year a group of black children and their parents brought a lawsuit to try to change the school segregation laws. This time all the Justices of the Supreme Court ruled against segregation. They said that public schools for whites and blacks could never be equal so long as they were separate.

School segregation was wrong and very harmful, the Justices said. Separate schools made black children feel different from white children. Separation made them feel that they were not as good as whites. When you don't think you're as good as other people, you don't learn as well in school.

Segregation, the Justices said, was bad for white children as well. The whites felt they were superior to blacks, and that was not true. The Court said that black and white children *are* equal and must be treated in the same way.

What did segregationists think about the Supreme Court decision?

They strongly disagreed with it.

— More than one hundred southern representatives and senators in the United States Congress signed a paper called the Southern Manifesto. In it they said that they believed in segregated schools.

— The Supreme Court had said that segregation in *public* schools was against the law. So some states closed public schools and opened *private* ones. States could then keep black children out of the white private schools.

— Prince Edward County in Virginia had no public schools at all from 1959 to 1964. For most of those years, one thousand seven hundred black children in the county had no schools to go to. Finally the Supreme Court forced the county to open the public schools again.

— Some whites were so angry, they joined groups called Citizens' Councils to fight for segregation. Others joined the Ku Klux Klan or other groups that believed whites were superior to blacks.

Members of these groups were often violent. They wanted to frighten blacks away from trying to exercise their civil rights. They burned crosses in front of black homes. Sometimes they destroyed the homes. So many black churches and houses were bombed in Birmingham, Alabama, that some people said the city should be called "Bombingham."

In the worst cases, these violent people would kidnap black people and hang them. When a person was killed this way, it was called a lynching. In the eighty years between 1882 and 1962, thousands of black people were lynched.

Most white southerners supported segregation, but some didn't agree with the violence. Very few, however, said anything. Only brave people speak up when no one else does.

Was segregation the same in the North and the South?

In the South, states and cities had passed laws saying that public places were to be segregated. In the North, certain neighborhoods or restaurants or clubs were segregated, but not by law. They were segregated by custom. Whites would say, "This is how we have always done things." That would be their excuse for keeping the races apart.

In the North, no laws kept black children and white children from going to school together, but few did. Blacks and whites lived in separate neighborhoods because many whites didn't want blacks in their areas. And schools were built where each group lived. In fact, Martin Luther King, Jr., went to Chicago in the summer of 1965 to protest against the very bad conditions in black schools.

In both the North and the South, black families

often lived in poor housing. And in both parts of the country, many stores and businesses wouldn't hire black people.

If you were black and you lived in a northern city, however, you were freer in many ways than if you lived in the South. You wouldn't have to drink water from a fountain with a sign COLORED ONLY. If you went to a lunch counter, you could eat next to a white person. When you boarded a bus, you could sit wherever you found a seat. If you went to the movies with your friends, nobody made you sit in a "colored" part of the theater. And in the North, your parents could vote in elections. In the South, almost no blacks were allowed to vote.

There was discrimination against black people all over the United States. But it was worse in the South. All the laws, all the ways people behaved, were meant to remind you that you were not as good as whites.

When did the civil rights movement begin?

The civil rights movement is the name given to the fight for freedom and equality for black people in America. Blacks have been fighting for their freedom since they were brought here as slaves more than three hundred years ago. But when people talk about the civil rights movement, they usually mean the protests in the 1950s and 1960s. During that time, thousands and thousands of people worked together to change the laws and customs that said white people were superior to blacks.

One of the first protests began in 1955 in Montgomery, Alabama. Thousands of blacks refused to ride the city buses for more than a year. They stayed off the buses because the bus company didn't treat blacks and whites equally.

The bus company lost a lot of money. This boycott of the buses was the first time that people all over the country heard about Dr. Martin Luther King, a young minister in Montgomery, Alabama. He went on to become one of the most famous civil rights leaders in America.

How did the Montgomery bus boycott start?

In March 1955, teenager Claudette Colvin refused to give up her seat on a bus to a white person when the driver ordered her to. She was arrested and taken to jail. Many blacks were very upset that a school girl had been arrested for standing up for her rights.

Nine months later on a Thursday evening, December 1, 1955, Rosa Parks, an adult, left her job at a department store to go home. She was happy when she found a seat on the bus, for she was very tired. The bus began to fill up, and soon there were no seats left. A white man got on. The driver turned around. He ordered a row of black people to stand up so that the man could sit. Three blacks gave up their seats. Rosa Parks didn't.

The police came and arrested her. They said she had broken the segregation laws. She had to pay a fine of fourteen dollars as punishment. Black people were angry that she had been arrested. Over the years other blacks had been arrested for violating the bus segregation laws. Many believed it was wrong that blacks had to give up seats to whites. They thought that people should sit wherever there were empty seats. And they wanted black bus drivers to be hired.

When Rosa Parks was arrested, Jo Ann Robinson and E.D. Nixon, two black people who lived in Montgomery, had a plan. They wanted to convince blacks not to ride the buses until the laws were changed. Jo Ann Robinson was the president of the Women's Political Council. The Council had wanted to boycott the buses for a long time. Ms. Robinson and others stayed up all night to print leaflets. She wrote:

Another Negro woman has been arrested and thrown into jail because she refused to get up out of her seat on the bus for a white person to sit down. It is the second time since the Claudette Colvin case. . . . Negroes have rights, too. . . . If we do not do something to stop these arrests, they will continue. The next time it may be you. . . . Don't ride the buses to work, to town, to school, or anywhere on Monday.

The next day she and her friends and their children distributed thirty-five thousand copies to blacks throughout the city.

Mr. Nixon telephoned black church ministers and community leaders. They held a meeting to discuss staying off the buses.

Many people heard about Rosa Parks' arrest because of the leaflet. And on Sunday, all the ministers talked in their churches about the plan for a boycott.

On Monday morning, empty buses rolled by Dr. King's house. Nearly fifty thousand black people had stayed off the buses. The boycott was a success! The black leaders met and formed a group called the Montgomery Improvement Association. They elected Dr. Martin Luther King, Jr., as president. That evening at a mass meeting, the black people of Montgomery decided to continue the boycott as long as they could.

How did people get to work or school?

Most people walked, some as many as fourteen miles a day. Others hitchhiked, rode bicycles, or shared car rides with friends.

Blacks went to their churches during the week and on Sundays for meetings about the boycott. The church was a place where many blacks felt at home. With their ministers they planned ways to keep the boycott going.

The black taxicab companies in the city charged people less than the usual fare for a ride. And people who owned cars picked up riders at special street corners.

People in other cities learned about the boycott from newspapers and television. Many sent money to help. Churches around the country donated station wagons.

The boycott lasted over a year. People were tired, but their spirits were up, for they were doing something to make their lives better.

One day one of the ministers said to an elderly black woman that she should use the buses, for she was too old for all this walking. She said absolutely not. "My feets is tired, but my soul is rested!"

What did the city officials and white people of Montgomery do about the boycott?

City officials tried to stop it in every way they could.

— They said that taxicabs had to charge the full fare, not a lower fare. This made it too expensive for most blacks to ride in the cabs.

— The officials said that car drivers couldn't pick up passengers because they were hurting the business of the bus company.

— Police arrested black car drivers for any reason they could think of. They said the drivers were speeding or didn't give the proper signals when turning. The drivers knew they were being arrested only because of the boycott.

— Officials called the newspapers and told reporters a false story. They said the boycott was over. They hoped that black readers would believe this and ride the buses the next day. But Martin Luther King and others learned of this plan and told the people in their church meetings that the story wasn't true.

Some whites called Martin Luther King's house and said terrible things to him on the telephone. Others became more violent. Dr. King's and Mr. Nixon's houses were bombed. Fortunately, no one was hurt.

Some whites supported the blacks. They gave them rides or helped them in their legal cases.

The Montgomery Improvement Association went to court and said that the whole system of segregation on the buses was illegal. When the case finally reached the Supreme Court, everyone waited to hear what the Justices would say.

Segregation on the buses, the Court said at last, was against the Constitution of the United States. The bus drivers could no longer force blacks to sit in the back or give up their seats to white people.

Friday morning, December 21, 1956, three hundred and eighty-two days after the boycott began, Martin Luther King, Jr., Rosa Parks, E.D. Nixon, and others boarded the city buses. They sat in the *front* seats as they rode downtown — and the whole country knew about it.

Does a protest like the bus boycott have a special name?

Yes. It is called nonviolent direct action.

Nonviolent means that the protesters would never use force to get what they wanted. They would only use peaceful ways. And they would never fight back, even if they were hit.

Some people think that if you don't fight with your fists, you are a weak person. Martin Luther King, Jr., always said that nonviolence is the way of a strong person, not a coward. It takes courage not to strike back. It takes strength to try to persuade people rather than hit them.

But how do you fight in a peaceful way against something you think is wrong? You can march with signs and hand out leaflets to let others know what you think. You can disobey a law that you think is unjust by sitting where you are not allowed to, or lying down and refusing to move. You can boycott, as in Montgomery. You can refuse to do something you're required to do.

All of these activities are also called *direct actions*. They are things you do, not just things you think about. You act in public so that other people will learn what you believe in. And you don't depend on others to fight for you.

Martin Luther King said you use nonviolent direct action so that people will pay attention to what you are saying. Writing a letter to a newspaper saying bus segregation is wrong is a good thing to do. But when fifty thousand people refuse to ride the buses until the law is changed, a great many people pay attention.

What were the sit-ins?

The sit-ins were nonviolent direct actions started by black students. Segregation laws throughout the South said that blacks couldn't sit at store lunch counters with whites.

On February 1, 1960, four black students from a college in Greensboro, North Carolina, went to the Woolworth's store in town. They bought a few school supplies and then went to the lunch counter. They ordered coffee and doughnuts.

"I'm sorry, we don't serve you here," they were told.

The students answered that the store had taken their money for the supplies. They said the clerk hadn't put their money in a box marked "black only." So why should there be a "white only" counter? They ordered again, but they were not served. They sat on the stools until the store closed.

Overnight the word spread to other schools. Within days, students in different cities were sitting-in at lunch counters in many different stores. By the end of February, there were sit-ins in thirty-one cities in the South.

Some white students joined the blacks. Together they filled the counter stools. So many students wanted to sit-in that they worked in shifts. You might sit at the counter for two hours and then someone would replace you.

Some white segregationists ignored the students. Others yelled at them, pushed them, or hit them. Some even poured water or ketchup on the students.

Young people in northern cities wanted to help the southern students. Woolworth's had stores all over the country. In the North, blacks and whites could sit together at the counters. But the northerners marched in front of the stores in their cities anyway. They asked people not to shop there until Woolworth's changed its rules in the South.

By the spring of 1961, segregation laws in stores and public places had been changed in nearly one hundred and forty cities because of the sit-ins.

Were there other protests?

After the sit-ins, people decided to try to integrate other kinds of places. Soon there were wade-ins at pools closed to blacks, stand-ins at segregated theaters, sit-ins at libraries that wouldn't lend books to blacks, kneel-ins at all-white churches, and lie-ins at hotels and motels that served only whites. People protested against every kind of segregation you can think of.

What were the Freedom Rides?

Among the most famous protests were the Freedom Rides. This time the law was on the side of blacks. The Supreme Court had ruled that long-distance buses traveling from one state to another could not be segregated. The stations where they stopped couldn't be either. But in most southern states, this law was ignored.

James Farmer was the head of a group called the Congress of Racial Equality, known as CORE. He thought up a plan to force the southern states to obey the Court rulings. In 1961, CORE announced that thirteen people — seven blacks and six whites — would begin a "Freedom Ride," starting in Washington, D.C., heading for New Orleans, Louisiana. The black and white CORE members planned to sit together throughout the whole trip.

The Freedom Riders were on two buses. Just outside the city of Anniston, Alabama, the trouble began.

The first bus was attacked by a mob of whites. They set the bus on fire and beat several of the riders.

When the second bus arrived in Birmingham, a crowd of screaming people beat the passengers as they got off. Some were very badly injured. People around the country saw newspaper pictures of the burning bus and beaten riders. They were horrified by the violence. The riders decided not to go on.

But a number of young people, mostly college students, felt that the Freedom Rides must continue. They believed that it was important to ride buses through the South until the buses were safe for everyone. They belonged to a group called the Student Nonviolent Coordinating Committee, called SNCC (pronounced "snick").

The students rode from Birmingham to Montgomery, Alabama. The next night, Martin Luther King, Jr., gave a speech supporting the Freedom Riders. An angry mob surrounded the church where he was speaking. Hundreds of people were trapped inside.

President John F. Kennedy was very upset when he learned about the attacks on the Freedom Riders. His brother Robert Kennedy was the Attorney General of the United States, the chief lawyer for the United States government.

Robert Kennedy tried to convince the governor of Alabama to protect Dr. King and the people in the church. When the governor refused, President Kennedy sent six hundred federal marshals to Montgomery. Finally the governor ordered the Alabama National Guard to break up the mob. Early the next morning, Dr. King and the others were at last able to leave the church.

The Freedom Riders continued their trip. When they reached the city of Jackson, Mississippi, they were arrested for disobeying the segregation laws in the station. All the riders were put in prison. Throughout the summer, hundreds more Freedom Riders rode buses into Mississippi and were thrown into prison.

At last, in September, the Freedom Riders won a big victory. The United States government made very clear rules about how to integrate the bus stations. This time, the rules were obeyed.

The words "Freedom Rider" became a badge of honor. During the years that followed, civil rights workers in cities and towns throughout the South were often called Freedom Riders. It didn't matter that some were teachers, or volunteers helping people to vote or giving out food and clothing. To many southern blacks, all people who helped them were "Freedom Riders."

Why did some protesters believe it was important to go to jail?

Most people think that only people who do bad things go to jail. But between 1960 and 1963 almost 20,000 civil rights protesters were arrested, and many of them went to jail. They hadn't stolen anything. They hadn't set fires or broken windows. They hadn't hurt anyone. What had they done wrong?

They had broken the segregation laws. This is called civil disobedience — refusing to obey laws you believe to be wrong, evil, or unjust.

It is a very serious thing to break the law. Civil rights leaders, like Martin Luther King, Jr., thought long and hard about what laws to disobey. Dr. King was arrested and put in jail in many cities throughout the South. When he was in jail in Birmingham, Alabama, he wrote a very famous letter that was published in newspapers and magazines around the country.

In his letter he said that all segregation laws are unjust because they hurt people. He said he didn't know how to explain to his six-year-old daughter why a public park was closed to colored children. He didn't know how to answer his five-year-old son, who asked, "Daddy, why do white people treat colored people so mean?"

When you break a law you believe is wrong, you accept the punishment. If that means going to jail, then you go. By sitting in jail you hope that people will begin to think and talk about the laws and understand why they are bad.

Martin Luther King and many others were put in jail in Selma, Alabama, for protesting against laws that kept most blacks from voting. Dr. King said that something was very wrong when there were more black people in jail with him than were allowed to vote.

Reverend James Bevel, who worked with Dr. King, told a group of young people, "You get an education in jail. . . . In the schools you've been going to, they haven't taught you to be proud of yourselves. . . ."

Many young people felt as if they were in honor classes when they marched for civil rights. Some carried their toothbrushes when they marched, just in case they were arrested and put in jail.

Were children involved in civil rights protests?

Yes. Young children, teenagers, and college students were all involved.

In early May, 1963, thousands of children protested in Birmingham, Alabama. Many of them were put in jail. Martin Luther King, Jr., had said, "Birmingham is probably the most thoroughly segregated city in the United States."

Dr. King was the president of the Southern Christian Leadership Conference, known by its initials SCLC. Some people in Birmingham asked Dr. King and SCLC to lead protests against segregation. The Birmingham protests began in April. But it wasn't until the children became involved that people paid attention.

On May 2, Dr. King spoke to hundreds of children at a church meeting. They were about to begin marching. Some were as young as six. The children left the church singing hymns and freedom songs.

The police began to arrest the marchers. So many children were arrested, the police had to use school buses to take them to jail. By evening, almost a thousand children had been arrested. The next day another thousand gathered to march. This time Police Commissioner Eugene "Bull" Connor had a plan.

He ordered the police to use attack dogs. And he told firefighters to turn powerful hoses on the marchers. Many of the marchers were knocked down by the water, and some were bitten by the dogs. All this was seen on television news. By the end of the day people all over the world knew Bull Connor's name and what he had done.

Some people thought it was too dangerous for young children to march. It was wrong to allow them to be jailed. But Dr. King said that black children were hurt every day of their lives by segregation. At least now they were standing up for themselves. They were saying to the world, "We are as good as everyone else."

Many people who saw pictures of the attacks on television realized for the first time just how bad segregation was. Bull Connor was the head of the police. He and his officers were not supposed to act like an angry mob. But they had. President Kennedy said, "What has just happened in Birmingham makes me sick."

Martin Luther King and others had talked to the protesters about the importance of not fighting back. But some people said Bull Connor's officers would never be stopped by the peaceful protesters. Then on Sunday, May 5, an amazing thing happened.

Two thousand people marched to pray outside the jail where the young people were locked up. When the police stopped them, they knelt to pray. Bull Connor ordered the marchers to turn back. But Rev. Charles Billups stood up and said, "We're not turning back. We haven't done anything wrong. All we want is our freedom . . . Bring on your dogs . . . Beat us up . . . Turn on your hoses. We're not going back!"

Connor yelled to his men to turn on the hoses. But no one moved. It was quiet in the street. Then the protesters rose and finished their march.

Within a short time the city's business leaders met with Martin Luther King and SCLC to work on a plan to end segregation in the stores. The "Children's Crusade," as many people called it, had made all the difference.

Were there special protest songs?

There were many of them. Singing was a very important part of the civil rights movement. Songs about freedom lifted everybody's spirits. Singing made you feel as if you were part of a large family. You felt strong and full of courage.

Sometimes people came to church meetings hours early just to sing together. In Selma, Alabama, third-grader Sheyann Webb often led the congregation in singing.

Protesters sang as they marched. And they sang while they were locked up in jails all across the South. The police and jailers tried to stop the singing. But they never could.

The civil rights movement in Albany, Georgia, became famous for its singing. The SNCC students there organized a group called the Freedom Singers. They traveled all around the country singing in concerts and raising money for the civil rights movement.

The protesters often sang church spirituals and hymns. Sometimes the words were changed so that the songs became freedom songs. When police or mobs tried to stop the protesters, they held their heads high and sang.

One of the best-known songs of the civil rights movement is called "We Shall Overcome." It became the national anthem of the movement. Today people all over the world who are fighting for their freedom know and sing this song.

What did segregationists say about the civil rights movement?

Segregationists always criticized the civil rights movement. Some said it was the "wrong time" for the protests. Black people should be patient. Martin Luther King, Jr., answered that it's always the right time to do what's right. Besides, he said, blacks have waited more than three hundred years for justice. He wrote a book called *Why We Can't Wait.*

Segregationists always looked for someone to blame. Often they said "outside agitators" — people who didn't live in the town — were stirring up trouble. "Our colored are happy," they said.

Dr. King answered that blacks didn't need anybody else to tell them that segregation was wrong. Black children and their parents knew that most whites wouldn't treat them as equals.

Sheriff Z.T. Mathews of Terrell County, Georgia, said, "We want our colored people to go on living like they have for the last hundred years." Many whites, like Sheriff Mathews, didn't want anything to change. Some liked thinking they were superior to blacks. But blacks were fighting against discrimination. The criticisms couldn't stop them.

What was the March on Washington?

On August 28, 1963, a quarter of a million people of all races traveled to Washington, D.C., from all over the country to protest against discrimination.

More than two thousand buses and thirty special trains brought people to the capital. On that sunny day, students, ministers, artists, secretaries, lawyers, truck drivers, cooks, writers, teachers, children and their parents — just about anyone you can think of — listened to Martin Luther King, Jr., and other speakers say that discrimination must be ended forever.

Two men, A. Philip Randolph and Bayard Rustin, planned the march. They worked with Dr. King and others from the civil rights groups. They said black people didn't have good jobs or schools or houses.

They said the government should do something.

President Kennedy announced that he wanted Congress to pass a new civil rights law. The civil rights leaders believed that the march would show the whole country and Congress that the time had come for equal rights for blacks.

Most people remember the March on Washington because of Dr. King's speech. He said, "I have a dream that my four little children will one day live in a nation where they will not be judged by the color of their skin, but by the content of their character."

Just a few weeks after the march, four young black school girls died in a bomb explosion set by segregationists in a Birmingham, Alabama, church.

What was "Freedom Summer"?

During the summer of 1964, almost a thousand students from the North went down to Mississippi. They went to work with the blacks who lived there. A young man named Bob Moses was a SNCC worker. He and people from two civil rights groups, SNCC and CORE, planned the summer program.

The civil rights workers set up freedom schools where poor blacks lived. They taught in churches, houses, and empty buildings. Everyone was welcome. Children ages eight to twelve studied reading, writing, spelling, math, and black history. Older students could choose different classes. They might study science or history or writing.

Voting was a big problem in Mississippi. Almost half the people in the state were black, but not one black had been elected to a government office. In fact, almost no black people were allowed to vote.

Whites often gave the excuse that black people weren't interested in voting. Blacks decided to show everyone that that wasn't true. In the fall of 1963 they set up their own "freedom" election to vote for governor. More than eighty thousand black people voted. Never again could anyone say that blacks didn't want to vote.

The real reason blacks didn't vote in Mississippi is that very few were allowed to sign up, or register, to vote. Whites had all kinds of rules to keep blacks from registering. Civil rights workers set up freedom schools to teach black adults how to register to vote.

Many whites in Mississippi were angry at the civil rights workers. The Ku Klux Klan burned churches and homes during freedom summer. Many blacks were arrested for trying to vote. Then something happened that made everybody in the country look at Mississippi.

On June 21, three young civil rights workers, James Chaney, Michael Schwerner, and Andrew Goodman, disappeared. A month and a half later, their bodies were found. They had been killed by a group of white men. One of the men was a deputy sheriff.

When their parents tried to bury the three together, Mississippi officials said no. James Chaney was black, and the state law said he couldn't be buried in the same cemetery as his white friends.

Some good things also happened during Freedom Summer. Since blacks weren't allowed to join the regular Democratic Party, they formed their own Democratic Party for elections. It was called the Mississippi Freedom Democratic Party. It was open to whites as well as blacks.

One of the leaders was a woman named Fannie Lou Hamer. She had worked on a farm for many years. One day she went to register to vote. Her boss told her to stop trying to register or she'd have to leave the farm. She left.

In the summer of 1964, the whole country learned about Fannie Lou Hamer. She spoke on television about how blacks were kept from voting. She spoke about how she was put in jail and beaten up by the jailers. And she spoke about the civil rights workers. She said, "They treated us like we were special, and we loved 'em. . . . We didn't feel uneasy about our language not be right. . . . We just felt like we could talk to 'em. We trusted 'em, and I can tell the world those kids done their share in Mississippi."

Did everyone agree with Martin Luther King?

All the civil rights groups and black leaders believed blacks and whites must be treated equally. But the groups often worked in different ways.

The oldest group, the National Association for the Advancement of Colored People (NAACP), was founded in 1909. It believed that the best way to change bad laws was to send lawyers to court. These lawyers argued that segregation was wrong. They won many important cases. In 1954 they convinced the Supreme Court to rule that school segregation was against the constitution. Thurgood Marshall was an NAACP lawyer who argued the case. Years later he himself became a Supreme Court Justice.

The Congress of Racial Equality (CORE) was founded in Chicago in 1942. Both blacks and whites were members. They believed strongly in nonviolent direct action. CORE organized the very first Freedom

Ride in 1947. CORE also started the well-known Freedom Rides of 1961.

Martin Luther King, Jr., and his group, the Southern Christian Leadership Conference (SCLC), believed in nonviolent protests. And they believed strongly in integration. SCLC was founded in 1957 by a group of black ministers after the Montgomery bus boycott. Dr. King was elected president. He traveled to many different places in the South to help local groups protest against segregation.

The Student Nonviolent Coordinating Committee (SNCC) was founded in 1960 by students from the sit-ins. These young people had very little money. They moved to poor black areas and spent a long time working and living with the people there. They set up freedom schools and helped many blacks to register to vote.

Malcolm X was a leader of a religious group, the Black Muslims. They worked in northern cities. At first Malcolm X did not believe in integration. He said that whites had done such terrible things to blacks that the two races should not live together. Blacks had a reason to hate whites, he said. In 1964, a year before he died, Malcolm X left the Black Muslims. He formed his own group and began to change some of his ideas.

He said his new group would work with anyone to end injustice to black people. He said he believed in a world "in which people can live like human beings on the basis of equality." And that was what all the civil rights groups believed in.

Why did Martin Luther King think voting was so important?

When Sheyann Webb was eight years old, she lived in Selma, Alabama. She went to a church meeting to listen to Martin Luther King and others talk about why blacks should register to vote. "If you can't vote, then you're not free . . . If you can't vote, then you're a slave," she heard one minister say.

If you can vote, then you can elect a police commissioner or a sheriff who doesn't turn attack dogs on children. You can elect a mayor who believes in integration. You can elect a school board that buys good books for all children. And when blacks began to register to vote, that's exactly what they did.

When John Kennedy was elected president in 1960, people realized how important black voters were. Kennedy and Richard Nixon were both running for president. People said the election would be very close.

Just before the election, Dr. King was arrested and put in jail for sitting-in with students at an Atlanta store. John Kennedy called Coretta King, Dr. King's wife. He said he would try to do what he could to help Dr. King. Newspaper reporters wrote about that phone call. On election day, a large number of northern blacks, who were allowed to vote, supported Kennedy. Many people said Kennedy won the election because of the black vote.

In 1965, in Selma, Alabama, Martin Luther King led protests about voting. Dr. King and others organized a march from Selma to the capital of Alabama in Montgomery. They wanted the governor to change the laws so that black people could register to vote.

The trip from Selma to Montgomery was fifty miles. On the first day of the march, the sheriff and his police stopped the marchers and beat them. President Lyndon Johnson, elected in 1964, made a television speech to the whole country. He said:

"It is wrong . . . to deny any of your fellow Americans the right to vote. Their cause must be our cause, too. Because it's not just Negroes, but it's really all of us who must overcome . . . bigotry and injustice."

At the end of his speech he spoke the words of the freedom song: "We shall overcome!"

President Johnson had helped to pass the Civil Rights Act of 1964. Now he urged Congress to enact a new law called the Voting Rights Act. It made illegal many of the things southern whites had done to keep blacks from voting. Because of this law, thousands and thousands of blacks have been able to register to vote. In 1982 President Ronald Reagan tried to take away this law because he said it wasn't needed anymore. But civil rights groups protested. They decided to march again from Selma to Montgomery in memory of the first march. President Reagan finally agreed to let the law stand.

Did the U.S. government help the civil rights movement?

Sometimes it didn't and sometimes it did.

The Federal Bureau of Investigation, known as the FBI, is part of the United States government. People who work for the FBI are called agents. FBI agents worked closely with southern sheriffs and police officers. Sometimes they knew beforehand that a white mob was planning to attack Freedom Riders, but they did nothing.

J. Edgar Hoover was the head of the FBI. Mr. Hoover said "outside agitators" were running the civil rights movement. He didn't like Martin Luther King, Jr. He said he was the worst "liar" in America. Mr. Hoover ordered the FBI to spend a lot of time investigating Dr. King, but not to spend time protecting civil rights workers.

But the civil rights workers believed that the government should protect them from people who planned to hurt them.

Often the presidents of the United States agreed. On several occasions, they *did* protect the protesters. They had to protect them against state governors who didn't believe in integration. Several times the presidents sent troops just to protect black students.

The first time was in Little Rock, Arkansas. In September, 1957, nine black students tried to go to the all-white Central High School. The governor of Arkansas sent the Arkansas National Guard to keep the blacks out. Then President Eisenhower ordered one thousand army paratroopers to Arkansas. He also used ten thousand soldiers. The soldiers walked the students into the school and to their classes for the whole school year.

In September, 1962, James Meredith, a black, tried to go to the University of Mississippi. The governor refused to let him enroll. President Kennedy was forced to send in federal marshals and the National Guard. For two days, white mobs fought the troops. But finally James Meredith entered the school. He became the first black to graduate from the university.

In 1963, President Kennedy again had to send troops, this time to Alabama. Governor George Wallace stood in the schoolhouse door to stop two students from entering the University of Alabama. Three thousand United States Army troops were standing by. Finally the governor stepped aside, and the black students entered.

President Johnson supported important civil rights laws. The laws were meant to end discrimination in jobs, housing, public places, and voting. These laws would never have been passed if there hadn't been a civil rights movement.

Did Martin Luther King fight only for civil rights?

Dr. King believed that all people should be treated equally and fairly. As a black person, he fought discrimination against blacks.

Dr. King also believed in peace. Civil rights protests should be nonviolent, he said. In 1964 he received one of the greatest honors a person can get — the Nobel Peace Prize — for his civil rights work. The prize is given to the person in the world who has done the most for peace that year. Dr. King said the honor was for the civil rights movement, not just for him.

Because he believed in peace, Dr. King also thought that the United States government shouldn't fight a war in Vietnam. There were so many people who needed help in America. We should be fighting against discrimination and poverty here, he said.

Just before he was assassinated in 1968, Dr. King had planned a Poor People's March to Washington, D.C. In the richest country in the world, he said, it's a sin that there are people who are hungry and homeless. He wanted blacks, whites, American Indians, Asian Americans, Mexican Americans — everyone — to join together in this protest.

Martin Luther King, Jr., was a leader for all people.

Was the civil rights movement successful?

One twelve-year-old boy who marched with the civil rights protesters in Selma, Alabama, said he was marching "for freedom . . . to go where you want to go, to do what you want to do, say what you want to say. I think we'll get it."

Americans did get many things from the civil rights movement. Laws were passed to end discrimination. Restaurants, hotels, theaters, bus stations, and other places can no longer be segregated.

Black people throughout the South can now vote. And blacks and whites have elected black congressional representatives, state government officials, city mayors, police chiefs, and others. In 1984 and 1988, many people of both races voted for the Reverend Jesse Jackson, a black man, for president of the United States.

Schools across the country teach about the history of black people in America. A black man has been a Justice of the United States Supreme Court. And Martin Luther King's birthday is a national holiday.

But success means other things as well. You can measure it by how you feel about yourself. Fighting for their own rights gave black people a sense of pride and dignity, a sense of being part of America.

Did the civil rights movement end when Martin Luther King was killed?

No, and Martin Luther King would have been the first to say that.

He always said that if he had never been born, there would have been a civil rights movement. There comes a time, he said, when injustice must end.

Violent people make a mistake when they think that they can end a fight for freedom by killing a leader. Dr. King said, "They can stop the leaders, but they can't stop the people." The civil rights movement was bigger than one person. It was made up of all people who believed in fairness and justice.

When thousands of people fight for freedom and equality, some will be hurt. Some may even die. Martin Luther King, Jr., was not the only person who died for freedom in the 1950s and 1960s. At least forty others also died.

After his own house was bombed in 1956, Dr. King said, ". . . If I am stopped, this movement will not stop. If I am stopped, our work will not stop. For what we are doing is right. What we are doing is just."

This was also true when others were killed. They died in the fight for freedom. And other people continued their work.

What's left to be done?

A ten-year-old southern black child was asked what she thought "freedom" meant. She answered, "Freedom means for your mother to get a better job, and for us to get better homes."

Many blacks have gotten better jobs and homes, but there are also many who haven't. When people can't get good jobs, they don't earn much money. Martin Luther King, Jr., always said that the battle isn't over when blacks can sit in a fancy restaurant.

They have to have enough money to be able to eat there.

Most whites in America have better jobs and earn more money than blacks. They live in better neighborhoods and go to better schools. More young white people go to college than blacks.

And there are still white people who are prejudiced against blacks. They have to learn that all people are equal and must be treated equally. Supreme Court Justice Harlan said the "Constitution is color-blind."

People, Dr. King would say, must also be color-blind in the ways they treat others.

WE SHALL OVERCOME

Moderately slow with determination

1. We shall o - ver - come, _____ We shall o - ver - come, _____ We shall o - ver - come some day, _____ Oh, ___ deep in my heart I do be - lieve We shall o - ver - come some day. _____

2. We'll walk hand in hand,
We'll walk hand in hand,
We'll walk hand in hand some day,
Oh, deep in my heart I do believe
We shall overcome some day.

3. We are not afraid,
We are not afraid,
We are not afraid today,
Oh, deep in my heart I do believe
We shall overcome some day.

4. We shall live in peace,
We shall live in peace,
We shall live in peace some day,
Oh, deep in my heart I do believe
We shall overcome some day.

Adapted from: WE SHALL OVERCOME, by Zilphia Horton, Frank Hamilton, Guy Carawan and Pete Seeger
TRO – © Copyright 1960 (renewed) and 1963 Ludlow Music, Inc., New York, NY
Used by permission. Royalties derived from this composition are being contributed to
The Freedom Movement under the Trusteeship of the writers.